DESTI**N**ATION

VANCOUVER

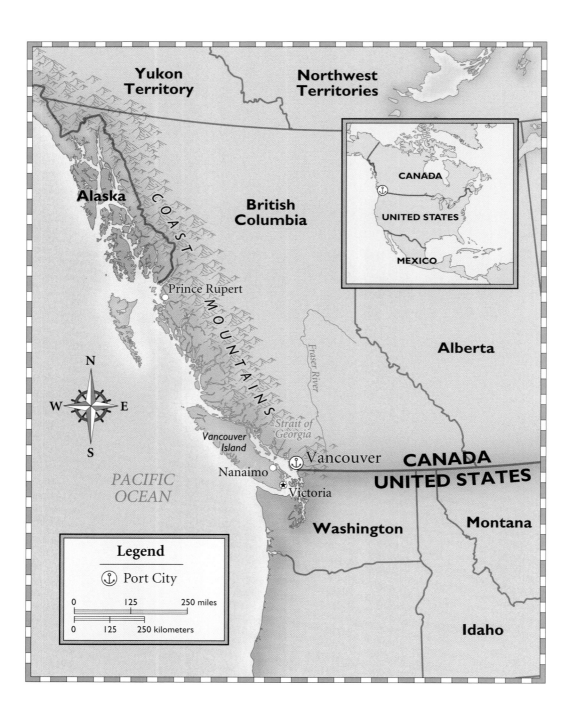

Yukon
Territory

Northwest
Territories

CANADA

UNITED STATES

MEXICO

Alaska

COAST MOUNTAINS

British
Columbia

Prince Rupert

Alberta

Fraser River

N
W   E
S

Strait of
Georgia

Vancouver
Island

Nanaimo

Vancouver

CANADA
UNITED STATES

PACIFIC
OCEAN

Victoria

Washington

Montana

Legend

⚓ Port City

0   125   250 miles

0   125   250 kilometers

Idaho

DESTI**N**ATION
VANCOUVER

by Lyn Hancock
with Guenther Krueger

Lerner Publications Company

PHOTO ACKNOWLEDGMENTS

Cover photo by © Thomas Kitchin/First Light. All inside photos courtesy of © Buddy Mays/Travel Stock, pp. 5, 17, 47, 55; Duncan McDougall/Diarama Stock Photos, pp. 6, 8, 10, 54; Wes Bergen/Diarama Stock Photos, pp. 16, 66, 70-71; Fred Chapman/Diarama Stock Photos, p. 57; © Gunter Marx, pp. 11, 22 (bottom), 25, 46, 52, 56 (top left), 60, 64, 74 (bottom); © Ken Straiton/First Light, pp. 15 (top right), 45; © Alan Sirulnikoff/First Light, p. 21; © Ron Watts/First Light, pp. 22 (top), 29, 48; © Thomas Kitchin/First Light, pp. 26, 69; © Robert Semeniuk/First Light, p. 56 (lower right); © Richard Hartmier/First Light, p. 62; © Peter McLeod/First Light, p. 67; © A. Griffiths-Belt/First Light, p. 68; Vancouver Port Corporation, pp. 15 (lower left), 18, 20, 27, 50, 61; © Robert Fried, pp. 19, 32, 73, 76; Corbis-Bettmann, pp. 30, 33, 37, 40; UPI/Corbis-Bettmann, pp. 43, 44; BCARS #A-04313, p. 35; McCord Museum of Canadian History, Notman Photographic Archives, pp. 36, 38, 39, 41; Neptune Bulk Terminals (Canada) Ltd., p. 51; Westshore-Ray Dykes Photo, pp. 59, 74 (top); © Lyn Hancock, p. 72. Maps by Ortelius Design.

This book is dedicated to Gerry Lavallee, with thanks.

LIBRARY OF CONGRESS CATALOGING-IN-PUBLICATION DATA

Hancock, Lyn.
    Destination Vancouver / by Lyn Hancock, with Guenther Krueger.
        p.   cm. — (Port cities of North America)
    Includes index.
    Summary: Discusses the geography, history, economy, and daily life of the port city of Vancouver.
    ISBN 0-8225-2787-1 (lib. bdg. : alk. paper)
    Vancouver (B.C.) — Juvenile literature. [1. Vancouver (B.C.)]
I. Krueger, Guenther, 1949–   . II. Title. III. Series.
F1089.5.V22H36 1998
971.1'33—dc21   96-48143

Manufactured in the United States of America
1 2 3 4 5 6 – JR – 03 02 01 00 99 98

The glossary that begins on page 76 gives definitions of words shown in **bold type** in the text.

CONTENTS

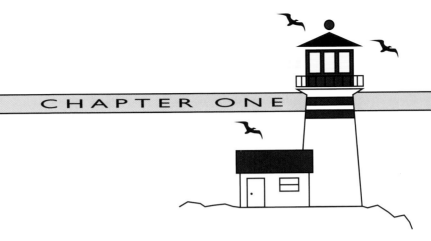

CHAPTER ONE

BY SEA, LAND, AND AIR

The Port of Vancouver is at the very heart of the city of Vancouver, British Columbia. In fact, you can't travel from one side of this Canadian city to the other without crossing some part of the port. That's because port facilities line the many waterways that surround this coastal city.

Location ➤ Vancouver lies in the southwestern corner of mainland British Columbia (commonly called B.C.), the westernmost province in Canada. The waters of the Pacific Ocean and its many inlets and channels form most of B.C.'s western boundary. A small portion of the U.S. state of

This marina in Coal Harbor (facing page) *shares the waterfront with commercial and passenger terminals.*

Alaska stretches along the province's north-western corner. B.C.'s northern neighbors are the Yukon Territory and the Northwest Territories—both part of Canada. To the east of B.C. is the Canadian province of Alberta. The states of Washington, Idaho, and Montana form B.C.'s border with the United States, which is only about 25 miles south of Vancouver.

The city is bounded by the suburban community of Burnaby to the east, by Burrard Inlet and English Bay to the north, the northern arm of the Fraser River to the south, and the Strait of Georgia to the west. Across this narrow **strait** is Vancouver Island, which shelters the city of Vancouver and its port from the Pacific Ocean. Forming a dramatic backdrop to the city are the peaks of the Coast Mountains. This range runs the length of B.C.'s coastline.

The Vancouver metropolitan area, known as Greater Vancouver, includes the city and its surrounding suburbs. The metropolitan area

Bounded by water on three sides, the city of Vancouver is surrounded by the many port facilities that line the area's waterways.

spreads across several **peninsulas** and islands separated by rivers, inlets, **fjords,** and bays. On a map, Greater Vancouver looks like the fingers of a hand pointing out to sea.

The Port of Vancouver includes facilities at Burrard Inlet, English Bay, and Roberts Bank—an artificial harbor on the Strait of Georgia. Several other ports also serve the city and its surrounding communities. Various port facilities, for example, line the north and south arms of the Fraser River, which empties into the Pacific Ocean at the Strait of Georgia.

The Port of North Fraser, which stretches along the north arm of the Fraser River, is too shallow for oceangoing ships. Instead it harbors small coastal freighters, fishing boats, tugs and barges, pleasure craft, float planes, and floating homes. This section of the river is also used to store logs that have been cut in the forests along B.C.'s coast. The logs eventually will be broken into smaller units for shipment upriver to inland sawmills. The Port of North Fraser is also an important connecting waterway to the deep-sea ports of Vancouver to the north and of Fraser Port to the south.

Fraser Port, like the Port of Vancouver, serves oceangoing ships and coastal vessels carrying cargoes such as cement, forest products, salt, sand, and gravel. Fraser Port also has two autoports for loading and unloading vehicles from roll-on/roll-off ships. These "ro-ro" vessels have ramps that lower directly onto the dock so cars and trucks can drive straight onto or off the ship. Fraser Port is one of the world's major import-export auto distribution centers, handling about 400,000 vehicles annually.

➤ The Port of Vancouver is run by the Vancouver Port Corporation, which is governed by a seven-member board of directors.

➤ The many arms of the Fraser River Delta, a triangular piece of low-lying land at the river's mouth, provide fertile land for farming.

➤ Fraser Port is home to the largest industrial area in B.C. and has more room to expand than the neighboring Port of Vancouver.

The automobile storage yard at Fraser Port's Annacis Terminals can accommodate 25,000 vehicles.

◄**Transportation Networks**

Excellent transportation networks link Vancouver to the rest of Canada, to the United States, and to the rest of the world. Canadian highways, U.S. interstates, and four railways connect directly to the port, while a large fleet of tugs and barges link B.C.'s coastal communities to the port. Vancouver International Airport provides a vital connection to Europe, to the United States, and to Asia. Cargo and passenger traffic to Asian countries is increasing every year, and the airport is expanding services and facilities to meet the demand.

Because of Vancouver's location on the Pacific Ocean, the city is known as Canada's Pacific Gateway. Except for Prince Rupert, B.C., Vancouver is the closest to Asia of any port or city on the West Coast of North America. The city's geographical location means increasing business for the port. Experts believe that by the year 2000, 60 percent of world trade will be with Asian countries. China, for example, has one of the world's fastest growing economies, and Vancouver was the first port in the world to set up an office there.

➤ Lions Gate Bridge is named for the Lions—two snowcapped peaks that rise to the north of the city.

➤ The Port of Vancouver is linked to four major railways—Canadian Pacific Railway, Canadian National Railway, BC Rail, and Burlington Northern/Santa Fe Railway.

An incoming freighter passes under Lions Gate Bridge, which marks the entrance to Burrard Inlet and connects Vancouver to the city's northern suburbs.

Description of the Port ▶ The Port of Vancouver covers 214 square miles of navigable waterways and more than 171 miles of coastline. Thanks to Vancouver's mild climate, work goes on for 24 hours, seven days a week, all year round, except for Christmas Day, New Year's Day, and Labor Day. Burrard Inlet provides one of the world's best natural harbors—safe, sheltered, ice-free, and deep enough that little or no dredging (channel clearing) is required.

All harbors are naturally protected. Burrard Inlet, for example, is protected by the First Narrows—a narrow waterway linking the inlet to English Bay. The bay, in turn, is sheltered from the Pacific Ocean by Vancouver Island and the Gulf Islands (a cluster of smaller islands in the Strait of Georgia). Natural rock barriers called breakwaters also protect the city's harbors by breaking the force of crashing waves.

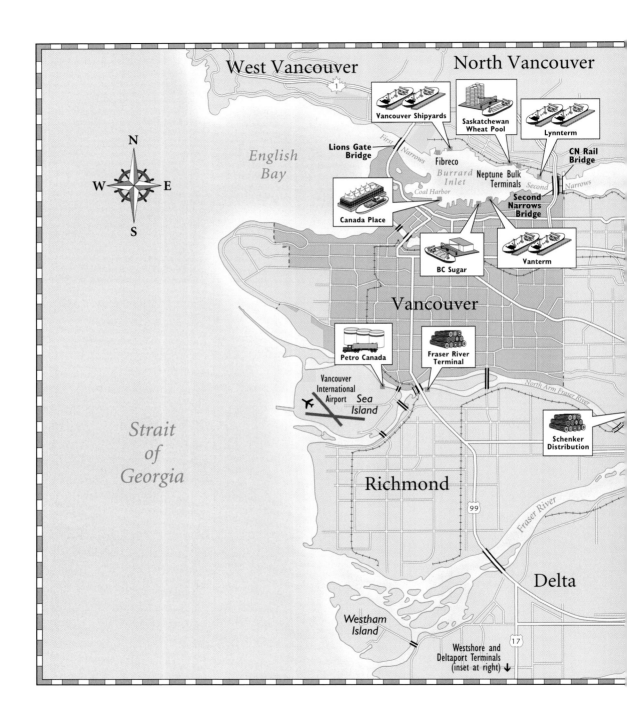

West Vancouver

North Vancouver

Vancouver Shipyards

Saskatchewan Wheat Pool

Lynnterm

English Bay

Lions Gate Bridge

First Narrows

Fibreco

Burrard Inlet

Neptune Bulk Terminals

CN Rail Bridge

Second Narrows

Coal Harbor

Second Narrows Bridge

Canada Place

BC Sugar

Vanterm

Vancouver

Petro Canada

Fraser River Terminal

North Arm Fraser River

Vancouver International Airport

Sea Island

Schenker Distribution

Strait of Georgia

Richmond

99

Fraser River

Delta

Westham Island

17

Westshore and Deltaport Terminals (inset at right) ↓

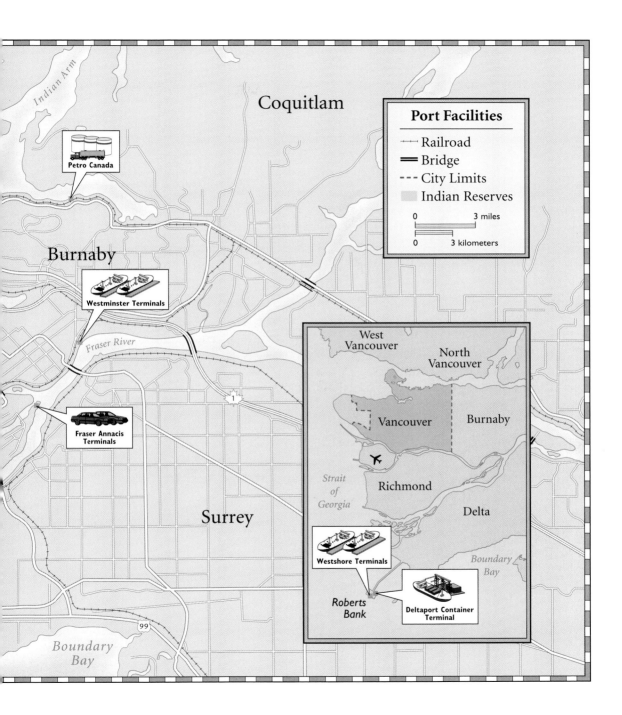

Coquitlam

Port Facilities

—|— Railroad
══ Bridge
- - - City Limits
Indian Reserves

0   3 miles
0   3 kilometers

Indian Arm

Petro Canada

Burnaby

Westminster Terminals

Fraser River

Fraser Annacis
Terminals

Surrey

West
Vancouver

North
Vancouver

Vancouver

Burnaby

*Strait
of
Georgia*

Richmond

Delta

Westshore Terminals

*Boundary
Bay*

Roberts
Bank

Deltaport Container
Terminal

*Boundary
Bay*

The barriers have other uses as well. Breakwaters off Point Grey (a peninsula jutting into the Strait of Georgia) enclose booming grounds, which are protected areas for storing logs and the scows (flat-bottomed boats) that carry them. And breakwaters off the Fraser River help accelerate the river's current, naturally scouring a deeper passageway for boats.

A variety of bridges, tunnels, and causeways (roads built over water) cross the many waterways of Greater Vancouver, allowing people to travel easily from one side of the metropolitan area to another. The Lions Gate Bridge spans the First Narrows in Burrard Inlet. To the east, the Second Narrows Bridge and the Canadian National Rail Bridge cross the Second Narrows. A speedy ferry known as the Seabus transports people across Burrard Inlet from the Canada Place terminal in Vancouver to suburban North Vancouver. Four bridges span the north arm of the Fraser River, while three bridges and a tunnel cross the south arm of the river, linking Vancouver's suburban communities.

➤ The average water depth between First and Second Narrows in Burrard Inlet is about 108 feet—deep enough so that no dredging is necessary. The shallow, silt-laden harbors of the Fraser River, however, require constant dredging to keep channels open and deep enough for ships.

◀ **Port Activity**

The Port of Vancouver is Canada's largest and busiest port. Based on the amount of cargo it handles each year, Vancouver regularly ranks among the top 5 ports in North America and among the top 20 ports in the world. Each year about 3,000 ships from 90 nations visit the port, which handled a record 71.8 million tons of cargo in 1996. This tonnage includes imports and exports that have both domestic and international destinations.

Vancouver is the most diversified port in the Western Hemisphere. It can handle everything

Grain (below) *is cleaned, graded, and processed at grain elevators before being loaded onto dry-bulk carriers* (right).

from coal and lumber to computers and cruise-ship passengers. Vancouver is the largest dry **bulk cargo** port on the West Coast of North America, handling more than 61 million tons each year. Among its most important dry bulk exports are coal, grain, wood chips, potash, sulfur, and metal ores. Top bulk imports (dry and liquid) include phosphate rock, salt, and fuel oil.

Some of the commodities that Vancouver handles are manufactured right in the port itself. Boats deliver fish such as salmon and halibut to the docks, where workers in fish-processing plants clean, fin, and can or freeze the fish. In 1995 the Port of Vancouver exported about 60,000 tons of fish and shellfish to markets around the world.

One of the oldest companies in the port is BC Sugar, which has been refining imported sugar from Australia since 1890. Along with another plant in Alberta, BC Sugar produces about one-third of the sugar sold in Canada. Workers at the port refine crude oil from western Canada and ship it as gasoline, diesel fuel, plastics, and other petroleum products to markets including coastal B.C. communities, the United States, Taiwan, Japan, and South Korea.

Petroleum products and other liquid bulk cargoes—including lubricating oils, liquid fertilizers, molasses, fats, acids, and solvents—are transported in parcel tankers. Like traditional oil tankers, these vessels are specially designed to carry liquid cargoes. But a parcel tanker has as many as 56 separate tanks inside its hull. This feature allows the ship to carry a variety of different liquid cargoes and to separate hazardous cargoes. Each tank is equipped with its own pumps and pipelines.

Vancouver is also a passenger port. Every year between May and October, luxury cruise ships head north to Alaska along the Inside Passage—a sheltered, scenic waterway between the mainland and the coast's offshore islands. In 1996

A dry-bulk carrier takes on sulfur at the Port of Vancouver. Bulk vessels carry their cargo in separate holds that lie beneath the deck. The largest bulk carriers can transport more than 91,000 tons of cargo.

cruise ships carried a record 701,547 passengers on the popular Alaska run. At other times of the year, cruise ships stop at Vancouver on their way to and from Asia, Hawaii, Mexico, and the Panama Canal in Central America.

Vancouver is known as a full-service port because it provides everything ships and their crews need. Small, maneuverable tugboats are available to push and pull giant cargo ships into position at a dock or to tow disabled ships to shore for repairs. At the port's large **dry dock,** vessels can be lifted, floated, or pulled completely out of the water for repairs and maintenance. Vancouver's shipyards build

The white sails of Canada Place mark the mooring area for cruise ships that visit Vancouver. The Vancouver-Alaska cruise is one of the world's most popular cruises.

ships. Service companies remove garbage, clean windows, or provide fuel. Ship **chandlers** pride themselves on being able to deliver a variety of equipment and international foods to ships around the clock.

Altogether the Port of Vancouver has about 20 major terminals and 79 berths for loading and unloading cargo and passengers. More are built every year as traffic at the port continues to grow. The terminals connect directly at the dock to a vast network of railways, highways, airways, pipelines, and shipping lanes. With the aid of ultramodern computerized equipment and highly skilled dockworkers known as longshoremen and stevedores, cargo can be moved quickly and efficiently between ships and other vehicles. This system of **intermodal transportation** helps ensure quick turnaround and speedy delivery of goods to market.

◄ Port Facilities and Trading Partners

Terminals specialize in different products and services. Seventeen terminals at the Port of Vancouver deal mainly with loose, unpackaged dry and liquid bulk cargoes, including coal, feed pellets, grains, fertilizers, minerals, chemicals and petroleum products, salt, and sugar. Some terminals concentrate on just one commodity, while others have equipment and facilities to move a variety of cargoes.

Most bulk cargo travels to Vancouver by railway. At the port, workers unload cargoes at docks and place them in storage facilities, such as warehouses, grain elevators, or tanks. Sometimes port workers load bulk cargo directly into

Vanterm (facing page), *one of Vancouver's 20 major terminals, has berthing space for five vessels and can handle a variety of cargoes, including containers. An extensive network of railways* (right) *links the Port of Vancouver to the United States and to the rest of Canada.*

the hold of a ship using conveyor belts, chutes, hydraulic loaders, and other computerized equipment. When cargo goes straight from a railcar or truck to a ship, it's called a direct hit. Direct hits are fast and allow cheaper handling of greater volumes of cargo.

The Port of Vancouver is a world leader in handling bulk cargo. Fibreco Exports, for example, operates the largest whitewood, wood-chip terminal in the world. Each year Fibreco handles about 1.2 million tons of wood chips, which are exported mostly to Japan. Westshore Terminals, located on an artificial island at Roberts Bank, is the largest coal-handling facility on the West Coast of North America. People often refer to Roberts Bank as a superport because its shipping basin is dredged deep enough and its dockside equipment is sophisticated enough to handle massive ships. Some

➤ About 83 percent of the Port of Vancouver's total annual tonnage is bulk cargo. Close to 11 percent is general (packaged) cargo, and the remaining 6 percent is containerized cargo.

➤ Some of the oceangoing vessels that stop at Roberts Bank are as long as three football fields and require a dozen tugs to maneuver into a berth.

Coal is loaded aboard dry-bulk carriers at Roberts Bank, the largest deepwater coal-handling facility in North America.

Onboard cranes lift general cargo off the docks and into the cargo holds of a vessel.

of these huge vessels can weigh as much as 275,000 tons.

At full capacity, Westshore Terminals can stockpile 3.5 million tons of coal at a time and can ship out 33.1 million tons of coal a year. The terminal has more than four miles of high-speed conveyor belts and four stacker/re-claimers to pile the coal and to reclaim it for loading a ship. Machines known as shiploaders can fill a ship with 15,400 tons of coal per hour.

Nine terminals at the Port of Vancouver handle **general cargo,** or items that are not shipped in bulk. General cargo includes forest products, such as lumber, plywood, pulp and paper, as well as iron and steel. These items may be packaged in bags, barrels, pallets, or cases, or they may be huge pieces of machinery that are hoisted directly on board a ship. General cargo terminals store goods in warehouses or open yards on the dock until the goods are ready to be shipped.

Shipping cargo in containers (above) *saves money because port workers can load large volumes of goods onto a ship very quickly. Containers mounted on wheels are rolled aboard ro-ro ships* (left) *through openings on the side or at the stern (rear) of the ship.*

A standard container is 20 feet long, or one TEU. Larger, 45-foot containers are increasingly popular with shippers, who can save money by transporting more cargo in a single trip.

High-value general cargo—such as machinery, computers, and perishable foods that require refrigeration—are transported in containers. These huge, closed, stackable metal boxes ensure safe and easy handling. Containerized shipping has increased tenfold since the 1970s and continues to grow. Certain cargoes such as specialty grains, which were once shipped in bulk, are now sometimes shipped in containers for extra protection against bad weather, theft, or physical damage.

The shipping industry measures container traffic in 20-foot equivalent units, or **TEUs,** because standard containers are 20 feet long. The Port of Vancouver has three container terminals, which together can handle more than 1 million TEUs annually. The port's newest container terminal is Deltaport. Completed in 1997, Deltaport is a 100-acre, two-berth site at Roberts Bank that is capable of servicing the world's largest container ships.

Automobiles arrive in Vancouver from Japan and South Korea in roll-on/roll-off vessels. Most ro-ro vessels head for the auto terminals on the Fraser River. These terminals have space to park the vehicles until they can be transported to market on trucks and trains.

The Port of Vancouver does much more than move cargo and people, manufacture goods, and build and service ships. It has seaplane bases, helicopter ports, yacht basins, and water taxi and seabus services. Marinas, hotels, restaurants, and parks are also located within the port. Houses, apartments, businesses, and Indian reserves (reservations) share the waterfront with ships, trucks, and trains.

Most cargo entering Vancouver comes from the United States, Togo (Africa), Mexico, Japan, China, and Taiwan. Almost all the cargo that leaves the port is headed for Japan, South Korea, China, Brazil, and Taiwan. Japan is Vancouver's biggest trading partner based on the amount of cargo shipped back and forth.

Ships coming into the Port of Vancouver must ◀ **When a Ship Comes In** make radio contact with traffic-zone officers of the U.S. or Canadian Coast Guard, depending on the ship's approach. To prevent ships from colliding, the vessels must report their name, position, radio call sign, and the time they expect to arrive at the Brotchie Ledge pilot station, just south of Victoria, B.C. Here, the ship picks up a B.C. pilot, who guides the vessel through local waters. The ships then exchange information about their positions by radio with Vancouver traffic officers at several established calling-in points along the route.

Captains follow special traffic lanes marked by a purple splash on their onboard charts and by buoys, colored markers, and lights on the water. From the Strait of Georgia, some ships will turn into Roberts Bank. Others head for the Fraser River, where a river pilot comes on board. The rest of the vessels, following the instructions of the port's harbormaster and the ship's agent, will anchor in the Strait of Georgia, in English Bay, or in Burrard Inlet to await docking instructions. Some ships are lucky enough to head right to a berth, where tugs help guide them into position. If there is no space, ships may be directed to the many safe anchorages in the nearby Gulf Islands.

Small, maneuverable tugboats help push and pull giant cargo ships into position dockside.

Oil tankers must obey special rules as they come into Burrard Inlet. For safety reasons, they have to navigate under Lions Gate Bridge one at a time. Tankers passing through the Second Narrows are only allowed to do so under certain tide and weather conditions, and they must be escorted by tugs.

To prevent pollution, wardens from the harbormaster's office inspect all ships entering the port. They seal the ship's engine room and discharge valves so that no pollutants are released into the water. The wardens also check the decks and **ballast tanks.** Oily water must be discharged onto slop barges, and sewage is treated either on board or at a nearby treatment plant. Workers collect and burn garbage so that disease is not brought into port.

The port uses a variety of machines to handle containers. Gantry cranes (left) *move containers on and off ships, while top-lifters* (facing page) *pick up containers from the top four corners and load them onto flatbed trucks.*

Dockworkers use a variety of machines to load and unload cargo. Bulk cargo, for example, is moved from ship to shore by conveyor belts, pipelines, or shiploaders. To handle containers, highly trained stevedores work giant **gantry cranes,** which may be mounted on rails or on rubber wheels. Smaller machines—such as top-lifters (which pick up cargo from the top four corners), side-lifters (which lift cargo from two side corners), and forklifts (which hoist cargo from underneath)—move containers, pallets, fish boxes, and bales of paper around the dock.

Workers must have good hand-eye coordination. In addition to learning to handle various types of equipment at a port training site, crane

◀ **Moving the Cargo**

operators practice moving containers on an ultramodern, million-dollar simulator. Trainees sit in a comfortable chair in front of a huge television screen. They use levers and switches to load and unload make-believe cargo. Although trainees are sitting in a classroom, they feel as if they were 50 feet up in the air, swinging from the dock to the ship's hold.

Many waterfronts consist of nothing but ships, docks, and factories. With towering snowcapped peaks, forest-covered mountains, rushing rivers, picturesque islands, and steep fjords, Vancouver boasts stunning scenery. It is one of the most naturally beautiful ports in the world.

AN EARTH-FRIENDLY PORT

Ports are often known for dirty air and water and poisoned fish and wildlife. Compared to other major seaports, however, Vancouver's ports are clean due to strict antipollution regulations. The Port of Vancouver, with its neighboring ports on the Fraser River, was the first in Canada to have a full-time department to enforce environmental rules and to look for new ways to improve the port's natural surroundings.

Running and maintaining a port can cause environmental damage. For example, log booms block sunlight needed by marine plant and animal communities. Dredging increases the amount of sediment in the water, clogging the gills of fish. The dikes (banks) and training walls on the Fraser River can destroy salt marshes, which act as sponges to soak up pollutants. The walls also increase the river's midstream current, which can make it hard for salmon to swim upstream to the spawning beds where they lay their eggs. And when a harbor is built or enlarged, some plants and animals lose their homes.

Port authorities try to make up for some of the lost habitats by providing plants and animals with new homes. Construction workers, divers, and biologists worked together to build artificial concrete reefs at Cates Park in Burrard Inlet and to design special concrete wharves at the Deltaport Container Terminal at Roberts Bank. Instead of building smooth-walled, concrete docks and pilings, workers punched holes in the concrete to make protected living areas for marine creatures.

Westshore Willy, a pilot whale from California, appreciates these efforts. For several years, he has been a regular visitor to the Westshore coal terminals at Roberts Bank. Willy reminds us that if we put our minds to it, industry and nature can coexist.

Bathers at Kitsilano Beach enjoy the clean water of English Bay.

At the Port of Vancouver, several beaches and parks greet ships at the entrance to Burrard Inlet. The waters around the Port of Vancouver and harbors along the Fraser River are popular recreation areas for rowing, paddling, sailing, and cruising in all kinds of boats. People also like to fish, hike, picnic, and watch birds along the waterfront.

Thanks to strict regulations and strong public interest, Vancouver's ports are among the most environmentally friendly in the world. Protecting the port's environment, providing up-to-date facilities and a well-trained workforce, and adapting to changing world trade patterns are all part of the effort to ensure the success of the port well into the twenty-first century.

CHAPTER TWO

FROM TREES TO CONTAINERS

Early Inhabitants ➤ Coast Salish peoples were living in winter villages along the shores of present-day Burrard Inlet at least 3,000 years ago. In the spring, summer, and fall, they set up fishing camps along the Fraser River. The Native peoples had front-door access to a variety of sheltered waterways and protected beaches to launch their canoes. Their back door led to mountains, forests, lakes, and lush river valleys.

The sea and the land provided everything the coastal peoples needed. They made tools, clothing, and dwellings from tall cedar trees. Hunters armed with bows and arrows, snares,

Ships anchor near a log boom (facing page) *in Burrard Inlet. Logging on the inlet helped Vancouver grow into a bustling port city.*

and nets tracked deer, elk, and bears. Berries and edible bulbs and roots were also collected for food. At sea, hunters used harpoons to spear seals and other water mammals. Fishers netted salmon, which were plentiful in the area's rivers.

Despite its dangerous currents and steep canyons, the Fraser River was an important trading route that linked coastal groups to the peoples of the interior. Coast Salish traders, for example, exchanged dried salmon and eulachon oil (fish oil) with the Interior Salish for copper, obsidian glass, sheep horns, and wool from mountain goats.

Through trade, coastal chiefs collected some of the rare and valuable goods they gave away at celebrations called potlatches. These ceremonial events were held to establish status and rank, to lay claim to certain powers and privileges, and to grieve the dead. Potlatches lasted

➤ At potlatch celebrations, some Coast Salish chiefs tore goat-wool robes into strips, which the chiefs tossed to commoners as a way of showing their authority.

➤ The Grease Trail was an important overland route used by Native traders who traveled between coastal communities and those of the interior. The trail got its name from the main item transported along the route—eulachon fish oil, a greasy substance that was eaten with dried fish to improve its taste.

Forests and waterways provided Coast Salish peoples with an abundance of natural resources.

several days and usually included fasting, dancing, theater, and gift giving.

Explorers and Fur Traders ➤ The Spanish explorer José María Narváez sailed into Burrard Inlet in 1791, becoming the first European to visit the inlet and to see the future site of the Port of Vancouver. Captain James Cook, a British mariner and explorer, had sailed by three years earlier while charting the coast, but he missed the forested, island-guarded entrance to the mainland. One year after the Spanish visit, another British captain, George Vancouver, explored the inlet as part of his own surveying expedition.

➤ Spanish Banks, a high bank at the entrance to Burrard Inlet, is named for Captain Vancouver's meeting there in 1792 with two Spanish sea captains.

As European explorers began sailing into the region in the late 1700s, Native groups started trading with the newcomers. The Europeans exchanged iron axes, nails, guns, mirrors, sugar, cloth, and whiskey for fish and furs from the Native traders. The two most valuable furs were sea otter and beaver, which the newcomers took back to Europe to be made into fashionable hats and coats. Over the years, Russia, Spain, Britain, and the United States competed for control of the new trading areas along the Pacific coast.

In the early 1800s, fur traders from the Hudson's Bay Company (HBC) of England and the North West Company (NWC) of Montreal worked their way across the North American continent looking for new trapping grounds and trading partners. They were also searching for a short, quick route to the Pacific coast. Traders hoped that one day goods could be transported to Europe by sea rather than by difficult and expensive overland routes.

Native peoples in the Vancouver region hunted and trapped beavers, sea otters, and other animals to trade with Europeans at local trading posts.

Along the way, fur traders built trading posts on convenient transportation routes and at spots where there were enough Native people willing to trap and trade. The HBC built its trading posts along the Columbia River, the only water route known at that time to lead from B.C.'s interior to the Pacific Ocean.

In 1808 Simon Fraser—a trader and explorer for the rival NWC—discovered another river route to the Pacific Ocean. But the explorer thought of this waterway, the modern-day Fraser River, as "a useless river." He named it the Bad River, not because its waters were treacherous, but because it did not lead to the Columbia River as he had hoped.

It wasn't until 1827 that the HBC (which had merged with the NWC) established a post on the Fraser River. Located near present-day Vancouver, Fort Langley was a trading post for fish and furs. Thirty years later, when gold was discovered upriver from Fort Langley near Yale, the company built another river post called Fort Yale.

Thousands of prospectors headed to the Fraser River to seek their fortunes in gold. By 1866 Britain had united the small trading settlements as part of the Crown Colony of British Columbia. New Westminster, a settlement on the Fraser River, was chosen as the colony's capital.

Fort Langley, established by the Hudson's Bay Company, was one of the first European settlements in the Vancouver area.

It wasn't fur or gold that gave birth to the port ◄
city of Vancouver. It was trees—tall, straight, coniferous (cone-bearing) trees, such as Douglas fir, red cedar, and hemlock. The trees, some of which grew 300 feet high and 12 feet across, thrived in the thick forests along the shores of Burrard Inlet and its natural, deepwater harbor. In the 1860s and 1870s, several little logging villages—including Moodyville, Hastings Mill, and Granville—sprang up along the inlet.

In 1864 the *Ellen Lewis* left Moodyville with a load of lumber and fence pickets bound for

The trunk of this tree provided a natural real-estate office for some of Vancouver's early entrepreneurs.

In 1885 workers completed the first transcontinental railroad in Canada, linking Vancouver to cities in central and eastern Canada.

➤ A devastating fire in 1886 burned most of Vancouver's buildings to the ground. Residents quickly set about building a new and better city from the ashes.

Australia. As news of B.C.'s tall trees spread, more and more ships came from around the world—Hawaii, Australia, China, and South America—to take on lumber from the forests around Burrard Inlet. The little port villages prospered.

In 1871 B.C. joined a confederation of four eastern Canadian provinces. As part of the agreement to become part of Canada, leaders in B.C. persuaded the Canadian government to build a transcontinental railway to link the province to the rest of the country. Thousands of Chinese immigrants came to B.C. to work on the Canadian Pacific Railway (CPR).

At first, the CPR planned to end the railway at Port Moody on the northeastern shores of Burrard Inlet. But in 1884, CPR general manager William Van Horne was so impressed by the deep harbor waters on the southwestern side of Burrard Inlet that he extended the railway 12 miles west to Granville in present-day downtown Vancouver. The Canadian government gave the CPR more than 6,000 acres of land at Granville. CPR surveyors set to work amid the trees and mudholes of the riverbanks to mark the streets and corners of a city that Van Horne prophesied would one day be "a great city in Canada."

Van Horne suggested that the village be renamed Vancouver, after Captain George Vancouver, to attract customers and investors from Britain. In 1886 the village officially became the city of Vancouver. The next year, the first transcontinental train crossed Canada and steamed into Vancouver to meet the SS *Abyssinia* from Yokohama, Japan. Dockworkers

Port workers unload tea from the Canadian Pacific Railway ship SS **Parthia.**

quickly loaded the ship's silk and tea onto the train. In a record-setting 21 days, the luxury cargo arrived in New York via Montreal. One week later, it reached London, England. Built by the CPR, these ships and trains—known as the Empress Ships and Silk Trains—were famous for many years for the speed and efficiency with which they transported silk, tea, passengers, and mail between Japan and Hong Kong and England.

THE EMPRESS SHIPS

Between 1891 and 1945, the Canadian Pacific Railway built the Empress Ships, beautiful steamships that plied the Pacific Ocean between Asia and North America. The ships and the CPR trains that met them dockside were famous for the speed and efficiency with which they transported silk, tea, passengers, and mail between Asia and Britain. No time was wasted. When the CPR ship pulled into the Port of Vancouver to unload, the CPR train was already waiting and steaming at the dock. Within 20 minutes, the last bale of cargo was stowed in the freight cars, and the train rolled away from the waterfront, speeding across Canada at the rate of a mile a minute.

During World War I (1914–1918) and World War II (1939–1945), when trade stopped between Britain and enemy Asian nations, the Empress Ships were pressed into service for the British Royal Navy. Two of the ships were bombed, one was gutted by fire, one was wrecked, and one was sold to an Indian prince. At the end of World War II, the CPR decided to discontinue its transpacific service. Much of Asia was recovering from the war and wasn't producing trade goods, so the CPR decided to bring the Empress era to an end.

In 1896 prospectors found gold on the
Klondike River in what became the Yukon Territory, to the north of B.C. Thousands of people from around the world dropped what they were doing and rushed to the northern wilderness to seek their fortunes. Many stopped first in Vancouver to buy food, clothing, tools, tents, lumber, and pack animals. Miners knew that the Royal Canadian Mounted Police were stationed in the Yukon to make sure that all prospectors had a year's worth of supplies. In Vancouver the prospectors bought everything they needed to outfit themselves for the long journey and the months, or even years, of working in the bush.

Miners en route to northern gold mines brought a lot of business to Vancouver, but only a few prospectors found the fortune they sought.

The Canadian Pacific Railway station in Vancouver bustled with activity in the late 1800s. Railroad lines connecting directly to the port allowed trains to meet ships dockside.

To meet the miners' demands, ships and trains rushed manufactured goods and raw materials to Vancouver. Shipbuilding, sawmills, and shingle mills thrived. Factories sprang up along the waterfront, and houses, shops, and offices mushroomed across the city.

By 1900 the boom in the Yukon had ended. The boom in Vancouver continued, however, as miners settled in the city to spend their newfound wealth. The expansion of railways also helped the port city to grow. In 1897, for example, the Canadian government gave money to the CPR to expand its lines on the condition that the railway reduce the cost of transporting settlers' possessions to the west. As a result, many people from eastern Canada took advantage of the lower rates to settle in Vancouver.

The opening of the Panama Canal in 1914 also helped the port city to grow. The new canal, which cut through Central America, shortened the sea voyage between European and Pacific markets by about 2,500 miles. No longer did ships have to go the long way

> At the end of the 1800s, Vancouver's population grew quickly, from 10,000 people in 1890 to 100,000 residents in 1910.

around stormy Cape Horn off the southern tip of South America. Faster transportation time meant lower costs, cheaper cargoes, and greater profits. With access to the new canal, the Port of Vancouver began exporting salmon and lumber to new customers in Europe and the eastern United States. To serve the increase in business, the port built additional terminals and a dry dock for ship repair.

During World War I (1914–1918), Vancouver's ◀ **The World Wars**
population dropped as many residents went to war overseas. But after the war ended, the port grew rapidly. Exports quadrupled between 1921 and 1929. To serve increasing grain shipments by huge bulk carriers, the port built more grain-storage elevators. Coastal steamship companies chose Vancouver for their headquarters. Eastern banks and businesses established branch offices and headquarters in the city. Factories and warehouses sprang up along the waterfront, and behind them rose fancy hotels and elegant mansions.

During the Great Depression—a worldwide economic downturn in the 1930s—banks failed, people lost their money and their jobs, and many businesses went bankrupt. People flocked west looking for work. But the port city, whose economy was also suffering, had little to offer. The economic situation didn't improve until World War II broke out in 1939. The movement of troops and wartime materials in and out of the port created new business. For example, war brought a demand for steel ships, so shipbuilding boomed in Burrard Inlet. In just two years, the number of shipyard workers

➤ Workers built the first bridge over the Second Narrows in 1925. Five years later, a freighter crashed into the bridge and destroyed the center span. In 1979 another freighter hit the bridge, which has been rebuilt and modernized several times in its history.

in North Vancouver alone rose from 800 to 12,000. Another 5,000 people worked in the Boeing Aircraft plant on Sea Island in the Fraser River. Other workers got jobs in factories making ammunition.

Bridge construction over Burrard Inlet also boosted the port's expansion. Before bridges, people had to travel by rowboat and steamboat to the sawmill, to the dry dock, and to the small community of Moodyville. The opening of the Lions Gate Bridge over the First Narrows in 1939 spurred the construction of homes and new businesses on the north side of the inlet.

Shipbuilding thrived in Vancouver and at other Canadian ports during World War II.

Postwar Growth ➤ World War II ended in 1945, and peace brought new customers from Pacific Rim countries that wanted to buy Canada's lumber, fish, coal, grain, and later, sulfur and potash. In the 1950s and 1960s, the Port of Vancouver sent large quantities of wheat to China and Russia. Coal, metals, oil, lumber, and other raw materials

were exported to Japan, which sent back manufactured goods such as radios, televisions, and
cars.

Vancouver was the first port in the world to
develop container traffic. In the 1950s, a company called The White Pass and Yukon Route
set up an efficient system of intermodal transportation to handle container traffic between
Vancouver, Skagway (Alaska), and Whitehorse
(Yukon). The company, which built the world's
first container ship, redesigned railcars to accommodate containers so they could then be
moved from ship to train (or from train to ship)
to complete the trip to market. White Pass containers carried everything from fresh tomatoes
to asbestos, lead, and zinc.

In 1970 a new facility opened on an artificial
island at Roberts Bank, near the mouth of the
Fraser River, to handle bulk and container traffic. And in 1986, developers built Canada Place

*In 1975 the supertanker
Amoco Cairo left the Port of
Vancouver carrying the
world's largest shipment of
grain. The grain was part of
a relief effort for Bangladesh,
a nation in Asia that was
experiencing food shortages.*

on the site of the old CPR wharves in downtown Vancouver. The project came just in time for Expo 86 (a transportation and communications fair) and for the city of Vancouver's centennial celebration. Canada Place, with its spectacular roof of sails, houses a convention center, a hotel, a world-trade center, and a cruise-ship terminal. The Seabus passenger terminal and the Skytrain rapid-transit station operate nearby from the old CPR station. Because of increasing numbers of tourists and businesspeople in Vancouver, developers are planning a hotel, additional convention space, and a third berth for cruise ships at Canada Place.

To serve Vancouver's ever-growing list of trading partners, particularly its Asian neighbors, Vancouver International Airport has expanded rapidly. Airline service to the United States and to Asian destinations has increased, and in 1996 the airport opened a new runway,

Ferry service is part of everyday life in Vancouver. The Seabus transports people from the Canada Place terminal in Vancouver to the city's northern suburbs.

terminal, and control tower. Through these expansions, the airport expects to add more than 1 million passengers and thousands of tons of cargo to its annual business.

Like Canada Place and the city's international airport, the Roberts Bank facility is also being enlarged and improved to handle increasing business. Workers completed construction of

Vancouver International Airport has become another arm of the Port of Vancouver, providing service for airlines carrying cargo around the world.

Deltaport, a 100-acre site for servicing the world's largest container ships, in 1997. The facility has a storage capacity of 13,000 TEUs. Four rail tracks provide space for two, 7,000-foot, double-stack trains. Deltaport also has a variety of dockside gantry cranes for moving containers onto and off huge oceangoing vessels. Additional units at Roberts Bank may eventually be used for cleaning and storing grain from Canada's western Prairie Provinces (Manitoba, Saskatchewan, and Alberta).

As a center of trade and commerce, Vancouver has become one of Canada's great cities.

The Future of the Port ▸ The Vancouver Port Corporation has developed a land-use plan called PORT 2010. To continue to be a successful and profitable port, the corporation believes it must do more than simply move cargo efficiently. In partnership with neighboring ports and municipalities the Port of Vancouver is working to protect the area's environment for the people and businesses of the twenty-first century.

The PORT 2010 plan stresses not only safe, efficient handling of cargo but also aims to improve air and water quality and to continue development of recreational and green spaces along the city's waterfront. In working to maintain Vancouver's reputation as one of the world's most beautiful and livable cities, port and city officials are upholding Van Horne's prophecy that Vancouver would one day become a great city in Canada.

CHAPTER THREE

GIVE AND TAKE

What Is Trade? ► Trade is the movement and exchange of goods from one place to another. International trade takes place among nations, while domestic trade is limited to trade within one country.

Nations trade because they have something that other countries need or want. Sometimes they trade because they can earn a profit by making something more cheaply than another country can. Often the importing country sells exports in return. A country maintains a healthy **balance of trade** when the value of its exports is higher than the value of its imports.

Canada exports more cargo than it imports. Altogether, about one out of every three jobs in Canada is linked to trade in some way.

A fully loaded container ship heads into Burrard Inlet (facing page). *The largest container vessels measure about 700 feet in length and some can carry over 2,000 containers.*

These railroad employees are just two of the thousands of people who help move goods in and out of the port.

Thousands of Canadians are employed across the country making, using, or moving the goods that flow through the Port of Vancouver. And since most Canadian trade goods travel to and from countries by ship, the Port of Vancouver plays a major role in Canada's economy. The port trades with more than 90 nations and handles more than 70 million tons of import, export, and domestic cargo, valued at almost 39 billion Canadian dollars (U.S. $29 billion).

The Port of Vancouver imports and exports **◄Imports and Exports** worldwide. The port's main trading partners are Pacific Rim nations. Goods leaving Vancouver go south along the coast to San Francisco and across the Pacific Ocean to Japan, China, South Korea, the Philippines, Australia, and New Zealand.

Ships that aren't too big to pass through the Panama Canal travel from Vancouver to Atlantic ports such as New York City, Halifax (Nova Scotia), and Montreal (Quebec). Some vessels cross the Atlantic Ocean to reach markets in Europe, the Middle East, and South Africa.

In terms of volume, the United States is by far the most important supplier of goods coming into Canada through the Port of Vancouver. In the mid-1990s, the port received about 1.1 million tons of cargo each year from its southern neighbor. Goods imported from the United States include fuel oil, gasoline, metal ores, sand and gravel, and manufactured items such as autos, heavy equipment, household appliances, office products, and steel. Because the United States is linked to Canada by a good highway system, many imported manufactured items and food products come into the country by truck and train.

A close second to the United States is Togo (Africa), which annually sends about 1 million tons of cargo (mostly phosphate rock) to Vancouver. In fact, phosphate rock (an ingredient in fertilizer) is Vancouver's biggest single import. Railway cars carrying potash from the

Dry-bulk carriers at Neptune Bulk Terminals discharge phosphate rock into freight cars.

Canadian province of Saskatchewan are unloaded at the port and then reloaded with the phosphate rock from Togo. The trains then turn around and head to fertilizer plants in the province of Alberta. No time or space is wasted.

In the mid-1990s, the Port of Vancouver handled almost 72 million tons of cargo annually, making it the biggest port in Canada in terms of tonnage and one of the top three ports in North America. Bulk exports, almost all of them from western Canada, accounted for 83.5 percent of this tonnage.

The port's biggest bulk export, in terms of tonnage, is coal. In 1995 more than 28.6 million tons of coal from Alberta and southeastern B.C. were shipped from Vancouver to Japan, South Korea, and 18 other countries. The Port of Vancouver handles 75 percent of Canada's coal exports.

This stacker/reclaimer at the Westshore Terminals loads coal onto a conveyor belt and into a ship's hold.

FUELING THE LIGHTS OF TOKYO

In terms of tonnage, coal is the single largest commodity exported from the Port of Vancouver. This mineral is a major source of energy for factories and power plants around the world. More than 29 million tons of coal leave the port each year for Japan, South Korea, Brazil, the United Kingdom, Taiwan, and Italy.

Miners extract coal in southeastern B.C., southern Alberta, and the western United States. The coal travels hundreds of miles to Westshore Terminals, located on a specially designed island at Roberts Bank about 32 miles south of Vancouver. The coal travels in open unit trains, which are sprayed with latex so the coal doesn't fly off en route.

Machines do most of the work unloading the coal trains at the port. The 112-car trains run on rails directly into a building where a rotary dumper flips two cars at a time, spilling the coal into a bin five stories underground. One person sits alone at a computer in the building to control the entire process. A conveyor belt then takes the coal to a giant, cranelike stacker/reclaimer, which sorts and stacks the coal into piles according to the type of coal a customer needs. To reduce coal-dust pollution, the piles are dampened with rain guns and high-mast sprayers. When the cargo ship arrives dockside, the stacker/reclaimer sends the coal by conveyor belt and chute to the ship's hold. Port workers must be careful to direct the coal evenly so that a good balance is achieved in the load. Coal ships can break apart while at sea if their cargo is not properly balanced.

In Japan the coal is used to produce energy for electricity. So when the lights of Tokyo go on at night, one of the sources of energy for the city is likely to be coal that was mined in Wyoming, Alberta, or B.C. and transferred from railcar to ship at the Port of Vancouver.

Trains line up at the Alberta Wheat Pool elevators to deliver their cargo. Freight trains carry grain to the port from the Canadian provinces of Alberta, Saskatchewan, and Manitoba.

Vancouver is also Canada's largest grain port. It handles 45 percent of Canada's grain exports, which rank second to coal in terms of volume. In 1995 port workers graded, cleaned, and processed about 13 million tons of grain at five large, 15-storied terminal elevators before loading the grain onto bulk carriers. Some specialty grains and animal feed are shipped in containers. Most of Canada's grain goes to Russia, China, South Korea, Iran, and Japan.

B.C. has the world's largest temperate rain forests, and about one-fifth of the province's workers earn a living from the forest industry. The province exports almost 30 percent of the world's softwood lumber, as well as large volumes of wood pulp, lumber, plywood, veneer,

➤ One million tons of bulk cargo is the equivalent of 100 trainloads of 100 railcars each.

➤ The Port of Vancouver handles 45 percent of Canada's grain exports. Sixty percent comes from Saskatchewan, while 35 percent originates in Alberta.

and newsprint. About 70 percent of these wood products go to the United States, while the rest is shipped to Europe and to Japan and other Pacific Rim countries.

Logging old-growth forest is very controversial, however. Many environmentalists want to leave forests alone. Workers in the logging industry, on the other hand, want to continue logging to protect their jobs and incomes. To strike a balance, lumber companies try to sell fewer raw materials, such as logs, in favor of

This newsprint plant on Vancouver Island is one of the largest in the world. Made from wood chips, newsprint is one of the many forest products that travel through the Port of Vancouver.

more finished wood products, such as wood paneling and veneer. These products are examples of value-added commodities—or raw materials that have become more valuable in monetary terms after being manufactured into a finished product. Economists compute this value as one way to measure and compare a region's manufacturing activity.

The Port of Vancouver exports more than 10 million tons combined of sulfur (left) *and potash* (below) *each year.*

Other exports handled by the Port of Vancouver include sulfur, which workers extract at natural-gas processing plants in B.C. and Alberta. The sulfur then goes to countries such as Morocco, Tunisia, and India for making fertilizer. Potash, another ingredient in fertilizer, is mined in Saskatchewan and exported to China, Japan, and other countries that use large quantities of fertilizer for growing crops.

◀ **Container Traffic**

Shippers use containers to transport a wide variety of products. The same container can move out of the port with one type of cargo and return later with another. Refrigerated containers hold perishable goods, while other containers can keep foods frozen on their way to a supermarket. Coffee from Colombia and bananas from Brazil come into the Port of Vancouver by container. So do car parts from South Korea and Japan that are destined for assembly plants in

The Port of Vancouver's highly efficient and versatile terminals have attracted container carriers from all over the world.

the eastern Canadian provinces of Ontario and Quebec. In the mid-1990s, 496,000 TEUs passed through the port each year—225,000 inbound and 271,000 outbound. The major goods exported by container include lumber, grain, animal feed, wood pulp, meat, and fish.

Protecting the ➤ Flow of Goods

The Port of Vancouver trades with countries all over the world. Many of these countries, including Canada, are organized into trading blocs, or groups of nations that trade with one another on a regular basis. The countries of the Commonwealth of Nations—which include Canada, Britain, Australia, and New Zealand—form one trading bloc. Canada has also formed a trading bloc with countries of the Pacific Rim.

Some port officials believe that future trading blocs will be increasingly regional. Trade among Canada, the United States, and Mexico is an example of a regional trading bloc. But whether trade patterns are regional or international, Vancouver is in an excellent geographic location to benefit.

To protect local industries, many countries restrict the flow of goods by putting up trade barriers. For example, a country may charge tariffs or fees on certain imported commodities to discourage local buyers from purchasing the imported goods. This practice helps protect local industries that manufacture the same products, by ensuring that consumers buy the cheaper, domestically made item.

To protect profits, nations sometimes place quotas on the production of certain goods so that fewer are available. Shortages, in turn, drive up the selling price and lead to increased earnings. Countries also financially support producers of certain kinds of goods. With these subsidies, producers can charge less for their products and earn more by selling greater quantities. On the other hand, some countries believe that trade should be free of tariffs, quotas, and subsidies. They think that if goods flow freely through a port, the products will cost less, consumers will buy more, and national economies will grow. One example of this policy is the North American Free Trade Agreement (NAFTA) negotiated by Canada, Mexico, and the United States. NAFTA, which took effect in 1994, phases out all barriers to trade in goods and services among the three countries over a period of 15 years.

> ➤ In the mid-1990s, the Port of North Fraser handled almost 19 million tons of cargo annually, including wood fiber, lumber, steel, and aggregate rock (for making concrete).

> ➤ In the mid-1990s, Fraser Port handled 25.4 million tons of cargo each year. Typical cargoes included autos, lumber, logs, wood chips, cement, aggregate rock, and steel.

NAFTA was designed to make it easier for the three nations to do business. Many experts believe that benefits occur as trade becomes freer. The Canadian government agrees and hopes that such benefits will include stronger earning power for some groups of Canadian workers, less unemployment, and increased efficiency in the movement of goods among the three nations.

Not everyone shares this point of view, however. Many Canadians feel that Canada is being overpowered by her more populous neighbors. Some types of products are cheaper in the United States and Mexico than they are in Canada, partly because the United States and Mexico have more consumers. In addition,

This worker at the Westshore Terminals performs routine maintenance high up on the arm of a shiploader.

wages in the United States and Mexico are often lower than they are in Canada, so production costs are also lower. For these reasons, U.S. and Mexican goods are often more attractive to Canadian consumers.

The value of money also affects how and what consumers buy. In some years, the Canadian dollar is worth less than the U.S. dollar. When the Canadian dollar is weak, Canadian goods are attractive to consumers in the United States because they pay less for Canadian commodities. Although there might be a demand for lumber and other Canadian goods, Canada would still make less money in the sale.

Even with NAFTA, certain trade barriers continue to affect some of the commodities moving through Vancouver's ports. The Canadian Wheat Board, for instance, is a federal agency that controls the sale and transport of grains grown in Canada. All Canadian farmers must

Freighters load lumber— one of Canada's most important commodities— in Vancouver Harbor.

Dry-bulk carriers line up at the Saskatchewan Wheat Pool in Burrard Inlet.

sell and transport their grain through this agency, despite the fact that it might be cheaper and less cumbersome to sell wheat directly to consumers in other countries.

Whether or not trade should be more or less restrictive is always under discussion. People working in industries that benefit from free trade favor agreements like NAFTA. Those who work in industries such as clothing manufacturing, which can be done more cheaply in Asian countries, tend to support government restrictions on imports and exports.

In general, customers want the best quality goods for the lowest possible price. Workers want the highest salary and the most benefits they can negotiate from their employer. Countries want good social programs and low unemployment to ensure a high standard of living. All of these forces interact and compete. They shift over time, as do priorities, technologies, and tastes. Trade, therefore, will always be in a state of change.

CHAPTER FOUR

THE PORT AND THE CITY

One of the most colorful terminals in the Port of Vancouver is the Saskatchewan Wheat Pool. The walls of the grain elevators that face the water are bright orange, giving a cheery welcome to oncoming ships. The back side of the elevators, which face houses in North Vancouver, are a quiet beige to please nearby residents. Being a port within a city means that the Vancouver Port Corporation and the privately owned companies that do business in the port try to get along with their neighbors.

The Port Corporation meets three times a year with mayors of the port's surrounding

The lights of the Vancouver skyline (facing page) *are reflected in Coal Harbor at dusk.*

Many people enjoy viewing shipping activity from Brockton Point in Stanley Park. The Vancouver Port Corporation has improved the quality of port life by adding recreational and green spaces along the city's waterfront.

municipalities to discuss and solve common problems. The corporation builds parks and diving reefs. It provides scholarships and jobs for students, and it sponsors the annual Picnic at the Port for children in the city's poorer communities. The corporation puts on a party when the first cruise ship arrives in the spring. And it organizes harbor tours and the annual Port Day festival, offering thousands of visitors free harbor cruises, displays, entertainment, and the chance to meet the port's mascot—a six-foot seagull called Salty Sam.

Vancouver is a friendly port. The Port Corporation has a bureau of speakers who give free presentations to the public on various port-related topics. The Vanterm and Lynnterm terminals provide public viewing areas for visitors to see the loading and unloading of ships. Vanterm invites thousands of school kids each year to tour its terminal and learn about its activities.

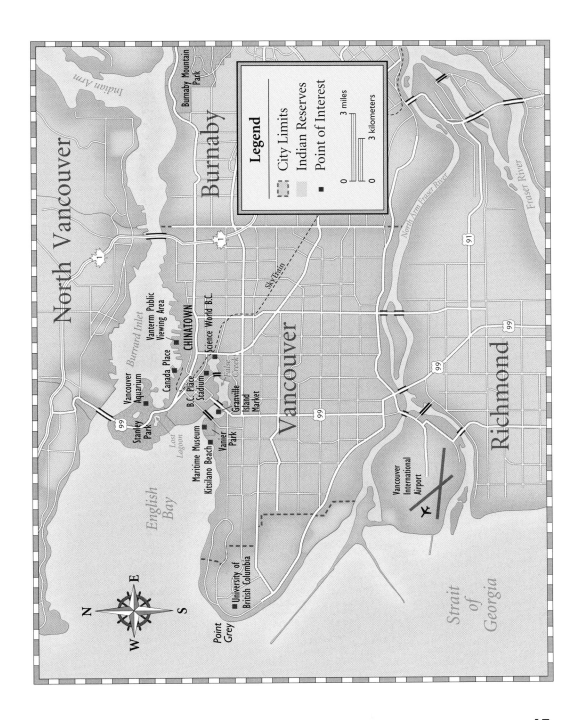

Indian Arm

North Vancouver

Burnaby Mountain Park

Burnaby

Legend

City Limits

Indian Reserves

Point of Interest

3 miles

0

3 kilometers

0

North Arm Fraser River

Fraser River

91

Burrard Inlet

SkyTrain

99

Vanterm Public Viewing Area

CHINATOWN

Science World B.C.

Vancouver Aquarium

Canada Place

B.C. Place Stadium

Granville Island Market

False Creek

Vancouver

99

99

Stanley Park

Lost Lagoon

Maritime Museum

Kitsilano Beach

Vanier Park

99

Richmond

English Bay

Vancouver International Airport

N

E

S

W

University of British Columbia

Point Grey

Strait of Georgia

A cosmopolitan city with a metropolitan population of 1.6 million residents, Vancouver has drawn people from around the world. Originally most settlers in Vancouver were of British origin and spoke English. This trend changed in the years after World War II, when many immigrants arrived from China, Japan, India, and Italy. By 1980 more than 40 percent of students in Vancouver's elementary schools spoke languages other than English. And by the 1990s, that figure had jumped to more than 56 percent. The main languages besides English are Chinese, Vietnamese, Punjabi, Spanish, and Hindi.

◀ **A Cultural Mosaic**

Totem poles in Stanley Park are a reminder of Vancouver's Native heritage.

The lion dance is part of the colorful parade that takes place during Vancouver's Chinese New Year celebrations.

➤ Vancouver residents cheer for the BC Lions (football), the Vancouver Grizzlies (basketball), and the Vancouver Canucks (hockey), the city's major professional teams.

➤ After high school, students in Vancouver have a choice of two major local universities—the University of British Columbia on Point Grey and Simon Fraser University in suburban Burnaby.

In the 1990s, about 23 percent of the people in Greater Vancouver were of British origin, while 16 percent had European roots. Another 15 percent of the population claimed Asian origins, although the number of Asian immigrants to the city is increasing. Native peoples make up about 1 percent of the city's population, while Latin American and African peoples together make up a little over 1 percent of Vancouver's residents. The rest of the population claim multiple ethnic backgrounds.

The foods, dress, building styles, customs, and festivals brought to Vancouver by various immigrant groups make the city an interesting place to live and to visit. Vancouver's Chinatown neighborhood is the second biggest on the West Coast of North America, after San Francisco. To celebrate the Chinese New Year, the Chinese community in Vancouver puts on a colorful parade and lion dance that wind through downtown streets.

Brightly lit boats tour Vancouver Harbor at Christmas.

Many celebrations take place right in the port itself. At Christmas brightly lit boats filled with carolers tour Vancouver Harbor. On January 1, New Year's Day, brave swimmers dash into the cold waters of English Bay for the Polar Bear Swim, to prove that Vancouver has the mildest winter in Canada.

The area's waterfront festivities attract large crowds. At the end of May, Vancouver hosts an annual Children's Festival. Performers come from around the world to play music, tell stories, and put on plays, dances, and puppet shows for young people. Events are held in Vanier Park, which overlooks English Bay.

The Marine Festival in the city of Nanaimo on Vancouver Island is famous for the World Championship Bathtub Race, held each July. In this competition, contestants race fiberglass copies of old-fashioned iron tubs that are powered by small outboard motors. The boaters start the race in Nanaimo and cross the Strait of Georgia to Vancouver, a distance of about 35 miles.

➤ Vancouver's weather is generally mild but rainy, with an average rainfall of about 47 inches every year. The average temperature in January is a balmy 37° F, while in July it's a cool 62° F.

➤ The Maritime Museum on Vancouver's waterfront displays the *St. Roch*, the first ship to sail the icy Arctic waters of the Northwest Passage both ways.

The six-mile seawall in Stanley Park is a place where people can stroll, jog, or sit and watch ships in the harbor.

My Kind of Town ➤ With a backdrop of mountains and many beaches and scenic waterways, Vancouver is often rated among the top 10 most beautiful cities in the world. It's also one of the few working ports in the world where the water is clean enough to fish and to swim in the harbor.

The city's most spectacular feature is Stanley Park, a 1,000-acre natural forest and recreation area at the entrance to the port. In the park, people can jog along the seawall, stroll the trails, visit the aquarium, feed the ducks in Lost Lagoon, eat at restaurants, play tennis, or just relax on the lawns.

Granville Island Public Market, located in Vancouver's West End, features theaters, art galleries, restaurants, and a variety of unique shops.

Away from the industrial port, Vancouver can be divided into two strikingly different areas. The affluent West End is known for its glass skyscrapers, beachfront apartments and other upscale residences, colorful markets, and gardens and parks. The East End, on the other hand, has a greater number of industrial sites and smaller houses on small plots of land. In recent years, many residents have moved away from the busy, crowded city to find more space and quiet in surrounding suburban communities such as Richmond and Surrey.

Vancouver is more than just a pretty seascape. Much of the city's success depends on money and jobs related to the Port of Vancouver. In 1995 the port contributed 1.68 billion Canadian dollars (U.S. $1.25 billion) to the nation's economy and paid about 500 million Canadian dollars (U.S. $373 million) in taxes to surrounding communities. (In Canada ports pay tax monies to citizens.) Vancouver's ports also benefit people all across Canada, from those who live or work at the waterfront to the wheat farmers, coal miners, lumberjacks, and other people who depend on the port to move their products to market. In addition, the port's workers have an economic impact on the communities where they spend their earnings.

About 10,700 people worked directly for the Port of Vancouver. Port employees include government traffic managers and the pilots and tugboat captains who guide ships into the harbor. The port also has longshoremen who load and unload vessels, port police, fireboat crews who battle fires, grain terminal employees who clean grain, and refinery workers who process oil and sugar.

Another 6,600 people work indirectly for the port in jobs related to the main businesses of the port. Crews drive trains, mechanics service machines, architects design boats, fishers haul in fish, and pilots fly planes or sail yachts. Other workers remove garbage from ships, greet and serve tourists at hotels and restaurants, and drive trucks.

In addition, more than 37,000 jobs depend on the water-related industries and port activities of the Fraser River. For example, more than

➤ Vancouver's suburbs include Surrey, Burnaby, Coquitlam, Richmond, Delta, North Vancouver, and West Vancouver.

➤ Tourism brings in at least 4 billion Canadian dollars (U.S. $3 billion) to Vancouver's economy each year.

40 wood-processing facilities are located in the Fraser River **estuary** and directly employ 9,400 people.

Many of the jobs generated by Vancouver's ports are service jobs in which workers provide a service rather than make a product. Service workers throughout the city include waiters, doctors, and tour guides, as well as the people who work in government offices. Altogether about 86 percent of the working people in Vancouver have service jobs.

Fish vendors are part of Vancouver's large service sector.

Another 8 percent of the city's labor force have manufacturing jobs in factories, making food products, beverages, machinery, plastics, printed materials, clothing, and telecommunications equipment. Construction jobs provide employment for another 5 percent of the workforce, while primary industries (agriculture, fishing, logging, and mining) employ only about 1 percent of all workers in the city.

At Westshore Terminals, two port workers (left) *monitor an operating program for a stacker/reclaimer. Although port work is becoming increasingly computerized and fewer workers are needed, port management and employees are working together to preserve jobs and to keep the Port of Vancouver running smoothly.*

Labor Relations ➤ Port workers and employers are organized into numerous associations and unions to negotiate a variety of job-related issues, including wages and benefits. Many employers at the Port of Vancouver are members of the BC Maritime Employers' Association. Dockworkers belong to Local 500 of the International Longshoremen and Warehousemen's Union. A number of additional unions exist for other types of port-related jobs.

Ports sometimes have labor problems, however. Work may come to a stop because managers lock out workers or because employees go on strike for better wages or improved working conditions. For example, more and more port work is becoming computerized, and fewer workers are needed to get the job done. Strikes sometimes involve negotiating to preserve jobs and to provide adequate training. Trouble between employers and employees at a port means that ships sit at anchor waiting to load or unload, and shipping companies lose a lot of money. The cargo vessels may leave to find another port. They may not return to the original port in the future.

Like other ports, Vancouver has had labor difficulties. But port workers and bosses are making a determined effort to cooperate and to work together without disruption. This is good news for companies wanting to do business at the Port of Vancouver. When employers and employees work as a team, customers know they can count on the port to operate smoothly year-round. And that's what the Port of Vancouver is all about. No wonder one of its mottoes is Keep It Moving.

GLOSSARY

balance of trade: The difference over time between the value of a country's imports and its exports.

ballast tank: A hold, or tank, deep within a ship that is filled with water or other heavy substances to keep the vessel stable.

bulk cargo: Raw products, such as grains and minerals, that are not packaged in separate units. Dry bulk cargo is typically piled loosely in a ship's cargo holds, while liquid bulk cargo is piped into a vessel's storage tanks.

chandler: A dealer who sells supplies or equipment of a specific kind.

dry dock: A dock where a vessel is kept out of the water so that repairs can be made to the parts that lie below the water line.

estuary: A water passage where the ocean tide meets a river current.

fjord: A deep, narrow inlet of the sea lying between steep cliffs.

gantry crane: A crane mounted on a platform supported by a framed structure. The crane runs on parallel tracks so it can span or rise above a ship to load and unload heavy cargo.

general cargo: Cargo that is not shipped in bulk. This category includes containerized and breakbulk (non-containerized, packaged) cargo.

intermodal transportation:
A system of transportation in which goods are moved from one type of vehicle to another, such as from a ship to a train or from a train to a truck, in the course of a single trip.

peninsula: A stretch of land that is surrounded by water on three sides.

strait: A narrow stretch of water that connects two larger bodies of water.

TEU: Twenty-foot equivalent unit. Container traffic is measured in TEUs. One TEU represents a container that is 20 feet long, 8 feet wide, and 8.5 feet or 9.5 feet high.

PRONUNCIATION GUIDE

Burnaby	BUHR-nuh-bee
Burrard	buh-RAHRD
Coquitlam	koh-KWIHT-luhm
Fraser	FRAY-zuhr
Montreal	muhn-tree-AWL
Nanaimo	nuh-NY-moh
Narváez, José María	nahr-BAH-ayth, hoh-SAY mah-REE-ah
Salish	SAY-lihsh
Saskatchewan	suh-SKA-chuh-wuhn
Vancouver	van-KOO-vuhr
Yukon	YOO-kahn

INDEX

METRIC CONVERSION CHART

WHEN YOU KNOW	MULTIPLY BY	TO FIND
inches	2.54	centimeters
feet	0.3048	meters
miles	1.609	kilometers
square feet	0.0929	square meters
square miles	2.59	square kilometers
acres	0.4047	hectares
pounds	0.454	kilograms
tons	0.9072	metric tons
bushels	0.0352	cubic meters
gallons	3.7854	liters

ABOUT THE AUTHORS

Lyn Hancock, originally from Australia, has lived in and traveled throughout Canada since 1962. She started her career as an elementary and high-school teacher and is now an award-winning photographer, lecturer, and writer whose books include *Winging It in the North, There's a Seal in My Sleeping Bag,* and *Nunavut* and *Yukon,* two titles in Lerner's "Hello Canada" series for young readers. Ms. Hancock lives in Lantzville, British Columbia.

Guenther Krueger is a freelance journalist and photographer. Based in Vancouver, he writes mostly about science and medicine.

ACKNOWLEDGMENTS

Lyn Hancock: I have lived in Vancouver for many years, but it wasn't until doing the personal research for this book that I realized how important the port is to our province and how interesting and friendly are its people. Work became fun as I cruised Burrard Inlet with the Harbor Patrol, monitored ships at the computer with the Traffic Patrol, watched a happy gang of longshoremen forklifting freight at Centerm, talked to visiting Polish fishermen taking on supplies near Portside Park, rode a stacker/reclaimer amid pyramids of coal at Roberts Bank, loaded make-believe containers onto a ship at the BC Maritime Employers' Association, and sipped tea while riding a paddlewheeler up the Fraser River to Fort Langley.

My thanks to the following people for making me feel so welcomed and for sharing their knowledge: Chris Badger, Steve Bushell, George Calhoun, Sam Chew, Dave Clausen, Darrell Desjardin, Raj Dholliwar, Maureen Dougherty, Captain G. B. Drewery, Ray Dykes, Evangeline Engelezos, Rand Flem-Ath, Lori Janson, Val Jones, Walt Judas, Karen Kelm, Captain Doug Leaney and Fraser River Connections, Graham Lee, Dave McMillan, Alain Mailhot, Linda Morris, Raija Oreva, Jacqueline Peacock, Gerry Peters, Brian Powell, Dave Quintell, Krishna Ralh, Pomponia Schmidt-Weinmar, Shamina Senaratne, Doug Sigerson, Dave Stephen, Dave Suttis, and Vicki Wong.

For always being there when I need you, thank you to Guenther Krueger, Gerry and Jo Lavallee, Cairine Powell, and Ivy Pye. And last but, of course, also first, my talented editor Domenica Di Piazza, who always makes my work fun.

Guenther Krueger: My thanks to Lyn Hancock for providing me with the opportunity to research and write this book, which was every bit as much fun as she describes. And I'd like to thank Barry Truax for his continued support and encouragement throughout my writing career.